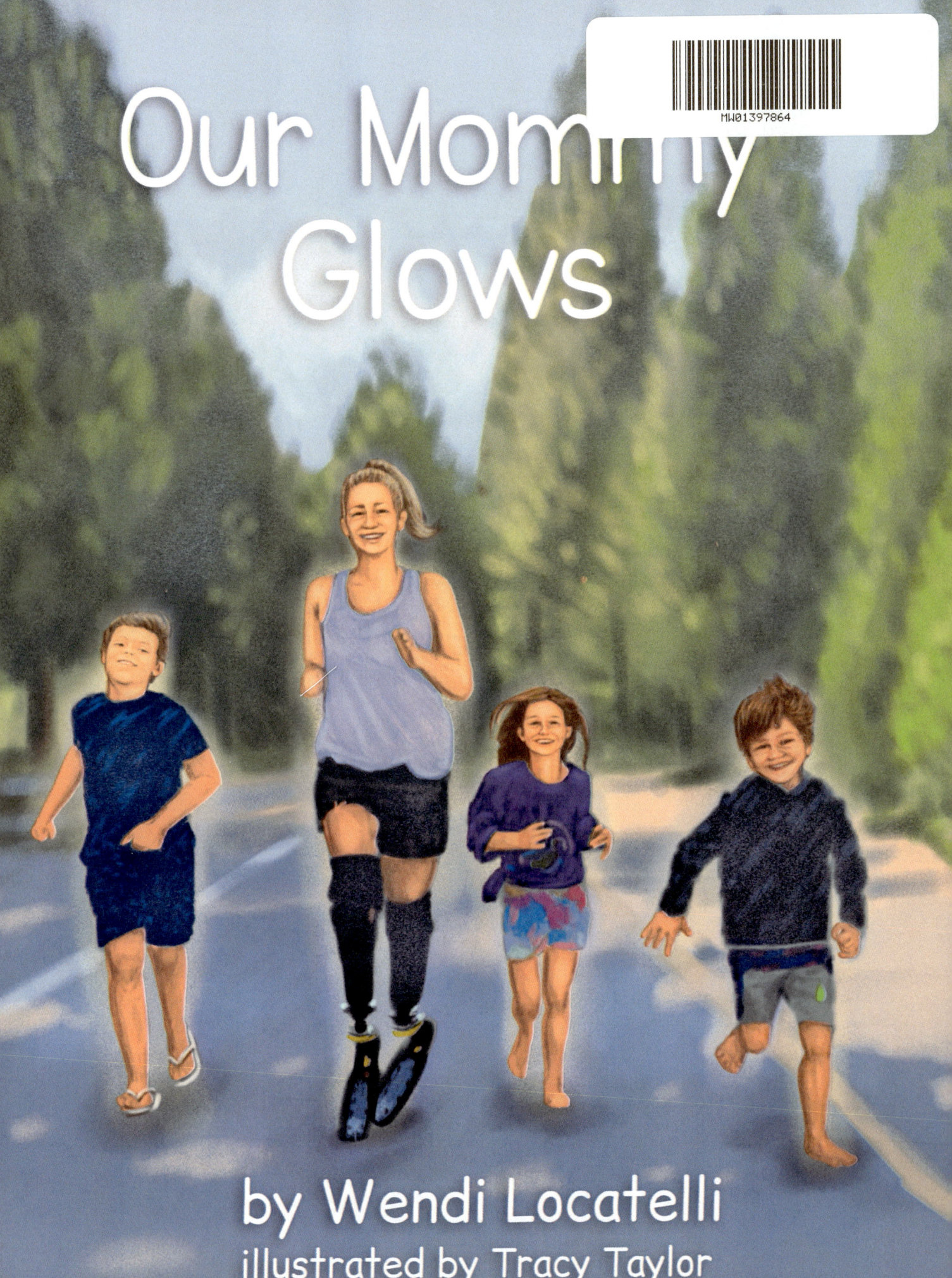

Copyright © 2021 by Wendi Locatelli

All rights reserved. This book or any portion thereof may not be reproduced or used in any manner whatsoever without the express written permission of the publisher except for the use of brief quotations in a book review.

Printed in the United States of America

First Printing, 2021

| Wendi Locatelli | Established 2021 | USA

Dedicated to Jay, Gage, Reed, & Drake,

You were and always will be my reason to live. Thank you for believing in the power of my spirit and remaining by my side during our darkest days. I pray that you never lose sight of your dreams and take every opportunity to live happily ever after.

Love,
Mom

This is our Mommy.

We think that she's amazing.
People say she

Glows...

But she gives
us all the
Praising.

She takes us on
Adventures,
exciting they
always are.

We are Amazed
at the places
she takes us
near and far.

We love to bake
together,
especially when it's
Cookies.

Sometimes we get
in trouble,
for licking all the
Goodies.

Mommy loves
to be in Nature,
and we do too!

We marvel at the
Animals,
as we take in
the view.

She likes to teach us new things, like Baseball, Art, and Swimming.

We trust her and do our best, right from the Beginning.

When it comes to Exercise,
our Mommy is so
Inspiring.

She shows us how to
work hard,
but we find it
very Tiring.

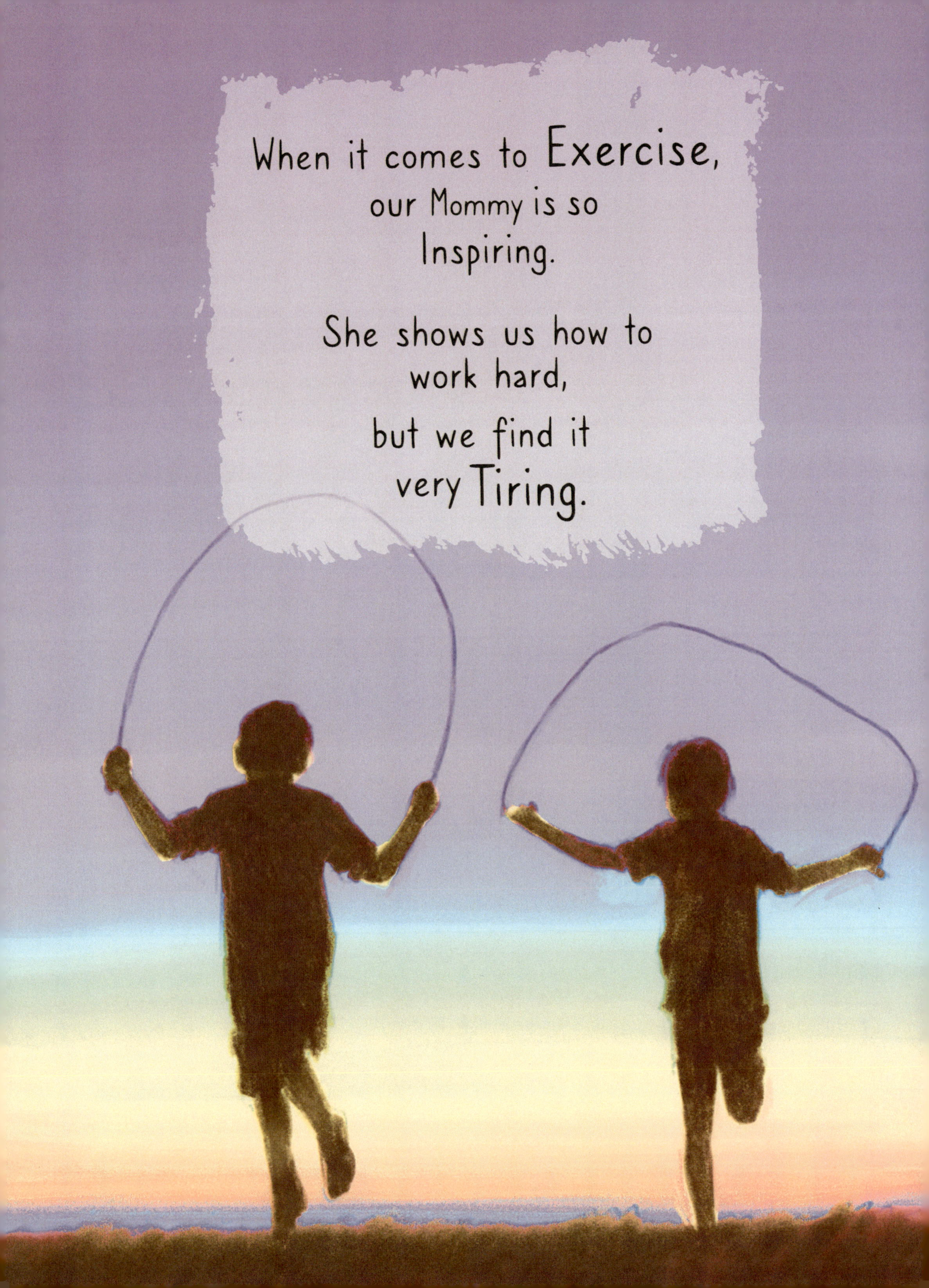

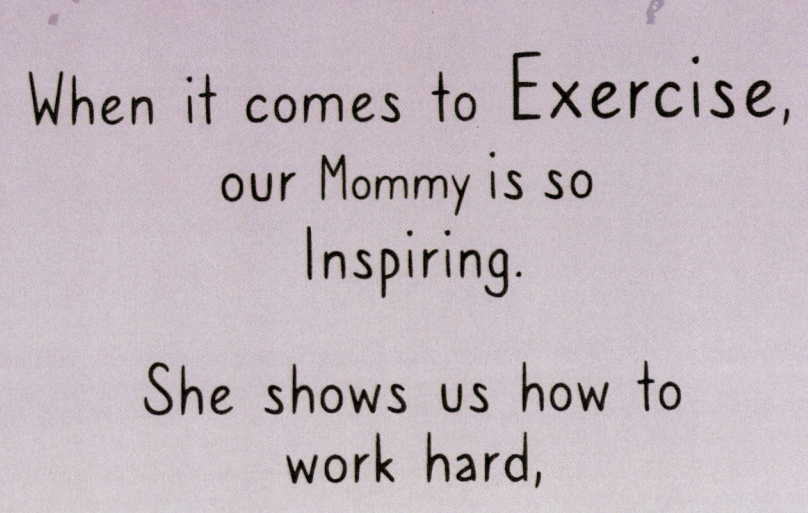

Cuddling is our favorite thing,
we do it every day.

It makes us feel special and loved,
in every single way.

One day Mommy wasn't home and we didn't know, why she had to leave us.

Did she have to go?

We went to visit
Mommy,
Daddy took us to the
Hospital.

The people there were
so nice,
They had done the
Impossible!

Mommy had been
Saved,
We are forever
Grateful.

We know that we are

truly Blessed

For everyone who

was Faithful.

We miss our Mommy so much,
and she misses us too.

We know that she'll be home soon,
but she still has lots to do.

Most importantly Mommy
is still here,
And that's what is the best!

Our job is to help and
support her,
This will be our life long test.

We're so happy
Mommy is finally home
We get to cuddle again.

It shows us

GOD

has a plan...

And for that we say amen.

Sometimes life changes,
Our Mommy is very
Brave.

She thanks us all the **time**
for the **love** that we gave
to make her **better**
and **help** her heal
From the inside out.

She couldn't have done it without us.
For that there is no doubt!

Mommy has a **robot arm**.
She has robot legs and feet.

All of the kids in our class,
Think it's **pretty neat**.

She still helps us,
and now we help her too!

We all work Together,
so that we make it through.

There are days that are Hard,
when we can all see,
that our Mommy is not,
the way, she used to be.
She may need our Help,
but is stronger in a way,

That we Appreciate,
with each new day.

Made in the USA
Las Vegas, NV
16 August 2023

76155984R00024